Full Scottish Breakfast

Graham Fulton

Red Squirrel Press
(Scotland)

First published in the UK in 2011 by
Red Squirrel Press (Scotland)

Red Squirrel Press (Head Office)
Holy Jesus Hospital
City Road
Newcastle upon Tyne
NE1 2AS
www.redsquirrelpress.com

Red Squirrel Press is represented by Inpress Ltd.
www.inpressbooks.co.uk

Cover photograph by Graham Fulton

Copyright © Graham Fulton 2011

The right of Graham Fulton to be identified as the author of this work has been asserted by him in accordance with Section 77 of the Copyright, Designs and Patents Act 1988.
All rights reserved.

A CIP catalogue record is available from the British Library.
ISBN: 978-1-906700-51-5

Printed by Martins the Printers
Sea View Works
Spittal
Berwick upon Tweed
United Kingdom
TD15 1RS

to Helen

Some of these poems have appeared before in the following magazines, newspapers, anthologies and online publications –

Cencrastus, The Glasgow Herald, Orbis, Ambit, Poetry Nottingham, Quattrocento, Scottish Poetry Library Best 20 Scottish Poems of 2006, Poetry Super Highway (USA), Blood Lotus (USA), Painted,spoken, Northwords Now, The Silt Reader (USA), Children, Churches and Daddies (USA), Snakeskin, Obsessed With Pipework, Nerve Cowboy (USA), Markings, Poetry Scotland, Brittle Star, Chapman, New Writing Scotland 23: Queen of the Sheep, New Writing Scotland 25: the Dynamics of Balsa, New Writing Scotland 26: Bucket of Frogs, The Eildon Tree, Fire, St.Mungo's Mirrorball Website, Neon Highway, Poetry Cemetery (USA), Skein of Geese: poems from The 100 Poets Gathering at StAnza 2007, Southlight, Earth Love, Southbank Centre Poetry Library Website

Contents

Space Age

The Movement of What's in the Sky	11
The Remarkable Love of Doctor McCallum	13
Classic Maths	15
Clone of Destiny	16
Joy Division	17
Silent Type	18
The Fireman on Hope Street	19
The Duke of Wellington on Queen Street	21
The Gospel According to Tiffany	22
Morning Dew on a Spider's Web	23
Remote Control Crawling Hand	24
The Gods	25

Rage Age

ID	29
Coffee Morning	30
Dark Age Rage	31
Dali Rage	32
Ballet Rage	33
On Loan Rage	34
Chariots of Rage	35
Delay Rage	36
The Outskirts of Paris in Edinburgh	37
Revolutions per Minute	38
Chihuahua	39
Empty	40

Middle Age

Respect for Your Elders — 43
Summer Student Carolyn Bruce — 44
Ticks — 45
Small to the Point of Vanishing Entirely — 46
Remainders — 48
Could Be a Ford Cortina But It's Hard to Tell — 49
Squirrels in Space — 50
Full Scottish Breakfast — 52
American Civil War — 54
The Life of Fergus in the Hall Cupboard
During the Very Wet Summer of 2007 — 55
The Death of Fergus on the Kitchen Floor
During the Very Hot Summer of 1976 — 57
The First Memory of Myself in the Sun
During the Very Long Summer of 1962 — 58

Space Age

The Movement of What's in the Sky

Apollo summer. Spacesuit first-foots
gathering rocks on pre-dawn telly,
sending seismic data to Earth.
The movement of what's in the ground.

We'd drive to where our time began –
the Oban road, Kilmartin Glen,
crammed with cairns and henges, cists,
astronomy swirls, hypnotic circles,
signs that shout out
        I am here.

Tolkien barrows, doorways to feel
the movement of the heat, sound,
the movement of what's in our heads,
decipher the language of dying, death.

We really weren't concerned with that.
We'd charge to the top of old Dunadd
and have a game of Japs and Commandos,
laugh at the edge at Craignish Point,
squint across the Firth of Lorne
towards the Gulf of Corryvreckan,
hoping to see a boat-sail pulled
below the whirling angry froth,
the silence of what's held beneath,
a sacrifice to some sad god.

We'd build our very own pagan cairn,
worship starfish, ancient crabshells.
Gape in awe at our tide-washed atoms,
shifting constellations in pools.

Eyes on the moon, spots on the sun.
Shape reflections.
        We are here.

At dark still sleepless, reach up to touch
the grown-up Armstrong and Aldrin world;
try to make out two little lifeforms
smiling back at two little lifeforms,
leaving prints on a bone dry sea,
walking on water that never was.

The Remarkable Love of Doctor McCallum

Doc McCallum had black hair
black-rimmed glasses   taught biology
    instructed us
in the way of the reproductive system
      the script of the Christian religion
belted everyone
at least once
on the palms of their hands
for talking in class   ignoring
homework
          loved to see
our hate
as he pulled the tawse
   from under his cape
      loved to scare
the lambs
by smashing it
on a stick of chalk
    at the edge of his desk
       for orgasmic effect

as we
watched the pieces
    exploding away
like the bang of a new universe
           he was
a god
   of wrath
         loved
to tell us
those who didn't believe
should be rounded up

          loved
to tell us
people from housing schemes
should be put to sleep
        in his spare time
loved to touch little boys
in the playground and bushes
until he was sent to prison
          we all cheered
      the school was demolished

Classic Maths

17:48 from Central,
creeping 17 minutes late.
A slow-mo pulling away from the shed.
A dreich removal beyond the outskirts.
Evening Times already read,
wedged tight down the side of the seat.

Motherwell station. Rain has stopped.
Five get off and three get on.
5 - 3 = 2.
The carriage inherently Arctic, numb.
Trolley, mental, arithmetic, magic,
gravity, Mars, momentum, nuts.

The laws for sense, sum of the square.
A father with his schoolwork son,
trying to keep his place in place.
Try to focus, izzy wizzy,
try to not get so distracted.
Think the end, create the start.

Carstairs Junction. Rain turns on.
This is one small part of our trip.
A slow-mo pulling away from the mind,
seagulls on a tall wire fence.
Three fly up and three fly down.
3 - 3 = 0.

Edinburgh, the long way round.

Rain-trails spawning across the glass.
We grind and groan and wheeze and arc
towards some kind of destination.
Try to not go off at tangents.
Understand, it's all we have.

Clone of Destiny

Some day I will go to Edinburgh
to see Dolly the Sheep at the Royal Museum.

Frankenstein muncher, superstar ruminant,
James Whale floozy, helix freak.
Boxed on a shrunken acre of soil,
a skimpy ration of virtual grass;
grazing amongst Industrial puffers,
coughing jallopies, cartoon machines.

The milestones of enlightenment.
Auld Reekie at the cutting edge.

It's alive! It's alive! said Colin Clive
as he winced at the stitched-up flatskull result
of mucking about with Hollywood brains.
The lightning zinged, the cameras rolled.
Today a cell, tomorrow a Man!

And what did you get out of it Dolly
before your date with the taxidermist?
Extra straw and early arthritis,
dodging a fate of mint sauce and carrots.

I know something you don't know.
The secrets of life, the age of God.

Post-modern Prometheus Holyrood geeks,
hooves in the footsteps of Bell and Baird.
We'll raise a dram to your DNA.
Scotland, as usual, showing the way.

Joy Division

In the GERMAN HISTORY part of the store,
nestling between the bestselling tomes
on Adolf's sex and Adolf's mind,
The Beginner's Guide to Cunnilingus.

Everything you could need to know –
minora, majora. I push it away,
fight to recall the reason I'm here,
sadness and hate on a worldcracking scale.

V2 rockets, life's too short.
What is a clitoris? Where to find it.
Strength through joy, death is a bore.
Advanced manoeuvres, flanking the spot.

I keep diving back for one more glance.
Picture the heart of the girl, I assume,
who placed it there to wake up my day.
Make love, not war, if you get the chance.

Silent Type

At the lights at the top of Union Street
a woman's bottom moons from the cab
of a big fire engine with helmets and bell.

Traditional alcohol-crawling rites.
A pink stretch limousine pulls alongside,
spunky one-night chauffeurs for hire.

Heat seeking hens traversing the road
combust as a twelve-inch-penised doll
is dirtily laughed from hand to hand.

Dreamstag, sized up, does what he's told.
Which Bride clones know who they want;
the measure of Man, helmet and balls.

The Fireman on Hope Street

A telepath birdcloud
                darts and dives
like Davie Cooper
                or Jimmy Johnstone
aeons ago,
        a feathered Old Firm
without the legless
                earthbound strips.

Taxis arrive,
                newspaper stands.
Santas bounce
                from Central exits,
wriggle and glide
                in the human Clyde.
A fairy inside
                a *Poundland* tiara
bursts her balloon
                and goes for a cry.
Not much older
                princesses wearing
summer in winter
                stagger in shivery
fishnets and basques
                towards the rank.
All of the anglers
                glued at the WAIT light
leap out their skins
                and twist their faces,
check what all
                the commotion's about.

Only the statue
              in black holds tight,
never allowing un-
                   planned-for bangs
to alter his breathless
                    gasmask view.
Endlessly eyelessly
                seeing up Hope Street,
patiently waiting
             for Glasgow to turn
to Baghdad, fireworks
                 to rip the sky.
A biblical hose
          to put out our fear.

The starling wingers
                dribble and jink
around the frostbitten
                 Christmas moon.
Taxis depart,
         the red man blinks
to green man walking,
                blinks again.
Bladdered waifs
          with arsecrack thongs
and reindeer antlers
             wave from the back.

The Duke of Wellington on Queen Street

There's a traffic cone
on top of his head
as he rides
     his aesthetic iron horse
outside the Gallery
   of Modern Art

          A Dadaist crown
for his statuesque hair
Vive La France! Napoleon Roolz!
The Auld Alliance
     is fine by us

We whack
    the history book in his face
as we pass on the way
         to a gastro pub
     a dive
on the Left Bank
of the Clyde

humming *La Marseillaise*
         and dipping
deep fried frogs
in tomato sauce

The Gospel According to Tiffany

On a Saturday city afternoon
a biblical shepherd, or Joseph,
in nativity clothes and real time beard
is standing outside a chock-a-block bookshop
shaking a not-very-full-up tub.

He's vying for our attention and change.
His tub is blue, he's shaking it for
a worthy cause – prevention of cruelty,
fly-covered Africans, heaven, light.

And inside the bookshop, under the bulbs,
Martine McCutcheon, Bow Bells babe,
is signing her I've-got-a-great-ass book
as men in the queue look down her top.

Her breasts are immense, her biro's a blur,
her teeth are as bright as the brightest button
sewn on the hat of a pearly queen.
Hello, how are you? Lovely to meet you,
thank you for coming, Happy Christmas.

And Joseph hasn't a ghost of a chance,
holy or otherwise, all he has
is faith in Man, the Book of his Lord.
Warm wool drawers beneath his sheet,
a dishtowel taped around his head.

Perhaps it's enough, we'll never learn.
Martine's limo purrs up to the door.
The Sally army precinct band
is blowing through *Silent Night* once more.

Morning Dew on a Spider's Web

Radiant droplets
galaxies   clustered   clinging
along the lethal silk
attached to the hinge
   of a cemetery gate

Subliminal trap to catch a fly
A perfect place to find a way in
        lose a way out
create a world

I crane my neck
for a graveseye view
   fumblingly think inadequate lines
to save this magic before it's gone –
       Aliens out
     of Wyndham stories
Fairy cocoons
   Snow Queen eggs

A perfect day to never have said
exactly what you know
should be said

A chandelier of tears is okay
Dribbles of souls on the beard of God
is nowhere near
        as far as I'll get

Remote Control Crawling Hand

You give me a beast with five fingers
        Made in China   green flesh
     Madeline Usher nails
   a hole in the stump
to place six expensive batteries
     a hand set
in the shape of a gouged eyeball
to make it jerk   very
slowly   across the endless steppe
of crumpled Christmas paper carpet

         watch it
clutching round and
round on the draining board
until it falls in the sink   knows
I am laughing at it   enjoy
the buzz of control   make it play
   an existential game of football
with santa   angel   nurse
on one side
      blow up doll   plastic fly
    on the other
   I get bored
switch it off
        leap
from my skin   as it gives
a series of twitches   residue impulse

goes for a walk
when I'm fast asleep   hoping
to find its box in the bin
the place it was made   reason it's here

The Gods

Gorbals saviour Alex Harvey
prowled the towering vertigo stage
of the sensational stone cold Apollo
with its bouncing Circle a mile in the clouds
    a benevolent incendiary mass
of friendly menacing energy
with his gap-toothed smile
    black-hooped shirt
        howled about Vambo   Isobel Goudie
            Delilah   The Chef
in December 1975
    explained the error of our ways
about hate   violence
    getting to heaven
    mixing the stew before it's too late
as Zal Cleminson strangled
platform-heeled riffs
from his spiky clown face guitar
at the Best
         Gig
            Ever

and the 4,000 cried out to be fed
    Alex punched through
his polystyrene burlesque tenement
with a stocking stuffed in his mouth
to let us know he was framed
again and again
as he flew too close to the sun
with his teacher's cane   buccaneer coat

and the Apollo
with its evil bouncers   honking toilets
    beer-slopped fag ash purple carpets
crumbled into bulldozer dust
like the traces of a proud civilisation
at the top of Renfield Street in Glasgow
    was replaced
by a cattle market happy hour dancespace
and superhero Alex fell to earth
with a heart attack in Belgium
because it's always too late

Rage Age

ID

At the ultimate *Marks and Spencer* till
the checkout girl with *Maureen* badge
confesses her name's not *Maureen* at all.

Maureen was spare, collecting dust.

Her till's the last one, down at the end.
Relentlessly cheerful, tearing off bags.
She lost her name, a long time ago.

Processed chips pile up on the belt.
We have to surrender to where we fit,
the easy ways we have to pay.

A badge in a box. A box in a drawer.

She wears her surrogate truth with pride,
a smile to tell us she's one of the tribe.
Would you like some cash back?
Pop in your PIN.

Coffee Morning
23/9/2006

In the hall beyond
                the yard of graves
the Dunblane children happily wait
to have their faces brushed with paint
by a girl who's almost
                twice the age
she would have been ten years ago.

A butterfly for a little lass.
Spider-Man for a little lad.

It's gone 9.30, the stalls are set.
A spark in a Barcelona top
is jamming a home-baked cake
                    in his gob.
Cubs are offering raffle tickets,
tablet squares and pots of tea.

The sun plays hide and seek on the floor
that's marked out for a netball court.
The three foot Ronaldinho sprints
the length of the hall and
                back again,
remains of icing, web on his skin.

Mothers chat, remember, together,
not to look at the clock and cry.
Strangers receive a second glance;
a man with a woggle collects
the token fee in a tub, it's 50p.

Dark Age Rage

In a gallery hung with Renaissance art
an iPodded boy in a *Road Hog* shirt
is emptily dragging his thumbnail across
some unprotected cerebral paint.

Tintoretto's *Ordeal of Tuccia* –
made it this far for hundreds of years
but met its match in a Glasgow twat.
You can hear the endangered figures scream.

Somehow, it wouldn't seem so bad
if he knew he was doing something wrong.
He's blank, his eyes are permafrost.
His nuclear mother and father, blank.

It's somewhere to go before The Mall.
They're probably taking him downstairs to prod
the dead stuffed elephant, Great Auk egg.
He'd loved to have pulled the trigger himself.

Dali Rage

At the foot of *Christ of Saint John of the Cross*
a man in a Seventies Soviet top
with CCCP in big white type
gets miffed as he tries to photograph
the immaculate oil on his *Virgin* Phone.

Excuse me he tuts to pensioner gangs
who shuffle his arty field of fire.
Worshippers keep on barging across
with buggies, crisps and *Somerfield* bags.

He turns an atheist shade of red.
He feels as if he's about to burst.

A small boy with a Roman helmet
squeezes and weaves his way to the front,
determined to get a place
at the crucifixion, Jesus without a face,

hanging a mile above the sea.
Everyone loves a madman with taste.
Forgive them Sal, they know not what
they do. Messiahs bring out the worst.

Ballet Rage

In the Theatre Royal Dress Circle bar
vultures are getting tetchy
as they try to order G & Ts,
dry white wines and Lite-sized beers.
Throats are on fire, women waggle
programmes like fans. Booze is required.

The men who want to be anywhere else
elbow their ground, splash their cash,
compete to impress their lifelong mates.

The barely-out-of-his-eggshell barman,
urgently unconcerned with pouring
overly-priced pre-tutu swally,
holds up £20 notes to the light.

The Bolshoi workrate is not for him.
All he desires is counterfeit Queens,
aggro, sweat, watching the thin
sophistication facade peel back.

Down in the *Swan Lake* orchestra pit
the bloke with the lonely triangle slowly
stares into space, prepares his ping.
Feathers are preened, the last bell rings.
The birds are on fire, the heating's on full.
Culture's an effort. Pain is required.

On Loan Rage

At the *Early Peoples*
    hands-off display
they're covering all
      the Pictish stones
with bubble wrap, Sello strips,
        hiding
all the unanswered language,
dumbing it down for
      going away.

A janitor with
    a forearm thistle,
needled with ink, whistling in tune,
     unwinds the tape,
  gags and binds
the story of
    our disappeared race.

Never mind, there's always
      the Scots
who fought to win, worked to remain,
    sprayed their claims
with poetry, chessmen,
hymnbooks, civilisation,
      words.

We'll soon forget,
    there won't even be
a trace like a badly removed tattoo.
He gets his cage and
    hauls them in,
wheels them, out there.
      Empty space.

Chariots of Rage

On the beach where
        Ian Charleson splashed –
   Vangelis and Liddell,
               arms, legs,
slowed to give
  an illusion
      of strength
                Royal   Ancient
             phantoms of sand,
    swept from dunes by mythic winds,
battering all that's left in their path:
golfballs, gulls,
    woman, her dog,
a dot, sun,   a mile long arc,
Antarctic flow,   St. Andrews in March
is not for the fragile of heart,
        the gods

uncompromising
       primordial rush,
wild,   perpetually
    moving walkway,
   meeting the North Sea tide head on,
equal, pure,   Olympus in Fife,
long dead actor,   heroes in shorts,
making the breakers bend and fizz,
nature surf upon itself.

Delay Rage

On the road between Dundee and Perth
greenfly hurl themselves against
the windscreens determined to end
                                    it all.
The opposite cars keep racing towards
the place we've left. We grind
                                    to a halt.

A bloke in the cab of a dozer
                              turns
his engine off and lights a fag.
A snake of cones uncurls
                              vanishes
into the distant high-strung clouds,
the limit is 40 m.p.h.

I scribble these lines on the face of a girl
kept in a dungeon for years by a monster,
man, a torn-off piece of *The Sun*.
Everyone wants to get to
                      everywhere else
as fast as they, possibly,
                            can.

A star with a Day-glo halo
                              hardhat
heaves a cross across his shoulder,
trudges towards the far green hills.
JESUS SAVES. EXPECT DELAYS.
A cow in a pasture empties its bowel.

The Outskirts of Paris in Edinburgh

In the annexe for Modern itinerant Art
an exhibition of Vincent Van Gogh
is packing them in at six quid a head,
not including the booking fee.

Cheap at the price, the madness is great.

Clots and splats, slapped on snots
of fever, tender ejaculations.
Shoals of sperms of violet, green,
yellow in yellow, spins of winds,
big bang grasses, revolvers of clouds.

Rivers of earth that flow in new
uncompassed directions, the usual crows,
blackly, above the flames of wheat.

We create the landscapes to help us die.

One in particular sucks me back
long after I've shuffled around the rest –
a blur-shaped outcast who's cut off his face,
trying to walk, escape from the frame
of bitterness, love, humanity, rage.

A wonky streetlamp, crimson roofs.

Unhappy air, the same old crows
no matter where I try to go.
The lighting is gentle, sane and soft.
I get the feeling we're being watched.

Revolutions per Minute

An Old Man of Hoy of 45s
and stacked-up LPs, mostly The Stranglers,
forged in the mists before CDs,
the dreadnought of punk, Atlantic of spit.

As *Down in the Sewer* ground through the speakers
The Dekester brought out his Falklands medal.
Thatcherite disc, Elizabeth hair.
It gleamed in the moonlight, I was impressed.

He told me how his mum and dad
believed he was dead when the *Plymouth* was hit.
They cried when they thought that he had died.
They cried when they heard he was still alive.
He had to clean the limbs from the deck.

He told me of a jolly jack tar
who spanked the monkey nine times a day,
another who used a special sock.
The Government kept us in the dark.

They can stick their medal up their arse
he said as he turned up *No More Heroes*,
this is what's real, this is what counts.

Peaches, Duchess, Jean-Jacques, Hugh.
The moon and Earth go round the sun,
the sun goes round what it goes round.
This is what this is all about.

Chihuahua

In *Gabriels* pub the match is on
a massive, plasma, wall-mounted screen.
Scotland have won the toss, Nil Nil.

A granny in a pink plastic coat
nudges beside us, takes a sip
of lager from her half pint glass,
tells us that she had to have
her dog put down this afternoon.

Ian thinks at first she said *Son*;
he may have misheard, the crowd is loud.
Scotland are holding on, we're calm.

I miss him a lot, he was just this big
she says, and demonstrates her claim;
a foot of space between her palms.
We try our best not to catch her eye.

It's nice to have … Ukraine have scored
in darkest Kiev, the clock ticks on.
We watch the drama of life unfold:
red offences, homer ref,
goal-line punts, theatrical dives.
He was thirteen, and had all his teeth.

A last minute penalty bulges the net,
she asks the barstaff to call her a cab.
Ian thinks at first she said *Son*.
He may have misheard, the time is loud.

Scotland are passing out, we're done.
I always fed him chicken and veg,
dog food's crap. Scotland are mince.

Empty

the crisp packet
with   no crisps
   in it is swept
from its place
             on the platform edge
    by the wake
of the cargo train
with   no cargo
on it is sucked
             suddenly in
to a darkness
                 is

Middle Age

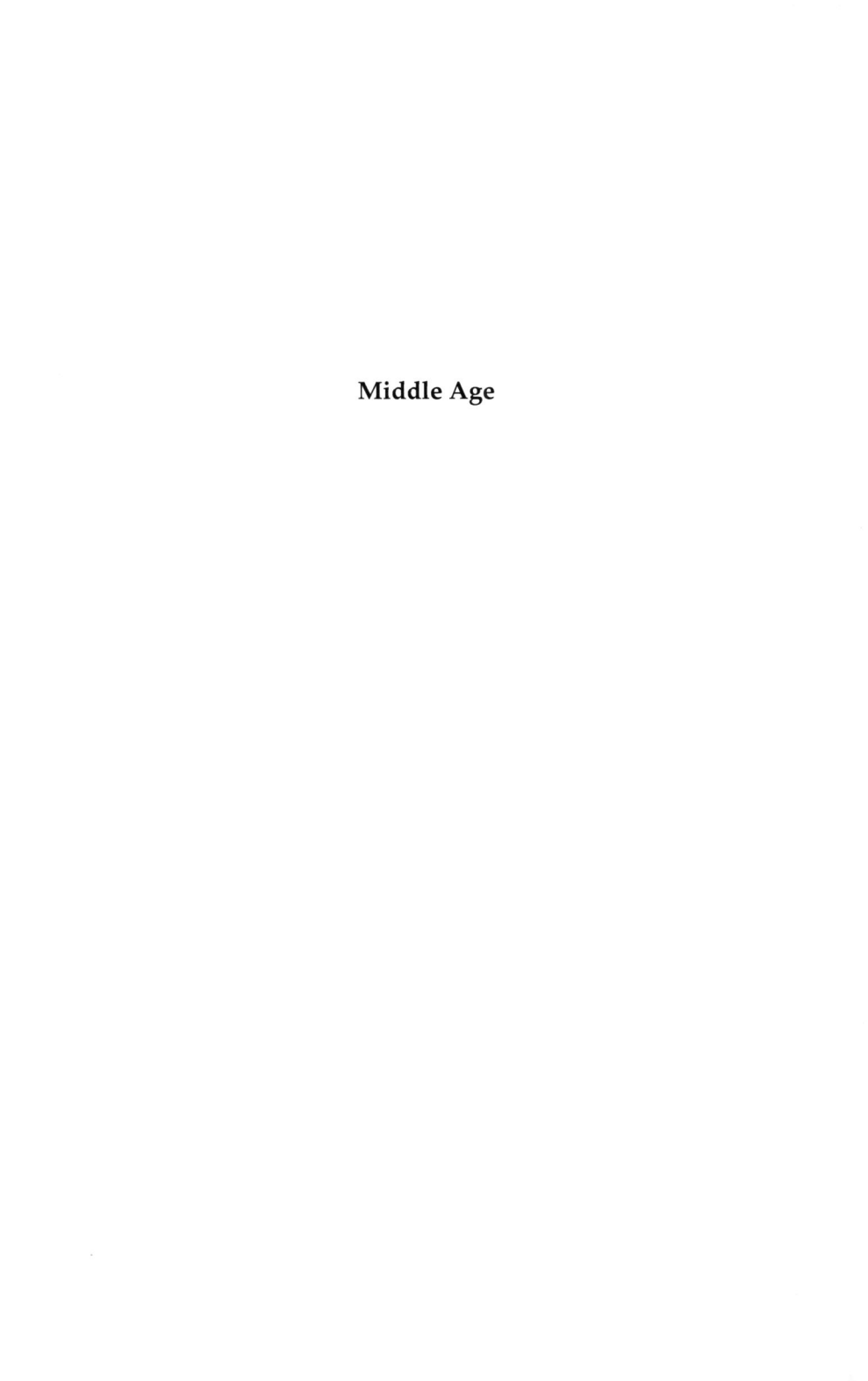

Respect for Your Elders

While rubbering home in a zigzaggy way,
   the fragile wake of a birthday pint,
a man was thumped on the back of his head
      by smiling babyface neds at a bus stop
trying to charm the girls they were with,
         arouse them with their bareknuckle moves.

The liquid refreshment had loosened his tongue,
            removed him from his guard for a while.
They'd belched a sneery jeer as he passed,
            replied with *Losers* – a bad idea.
Down on his stern like a brick Titanic.
         Something to do as they stood at the stop.

Kicks meteored in about his brain
            as he cringed, foetus-like,
in womb-wet slush.
After a while they got a bit bored,
         forgot the assault and jumped their bus.
It could have been worse, they failed to break
      the Chilean red in his *ASDA* bag.

Congratulations! Forty today!
   Muggers get younger all the time,
just like doctors and policemen,
said a wee granny who helped him stand,
fished for tissues inside her coat.

He didn't know whether to laugh or
cry. So he cried.

Summer Student Carolyn Bruce

The only picture of you I have.
Bottom left corner, short hair, coat,
back to the camera, better than me.
           Something else, a soul,
I guess.
You worked all summer, laughed a lot,
said *Goodbye, I'll be in touch.*
      We caught the whisper *Carolyn's gone,*
she died in a crash on her way
to church.

We chipped in for a bunch of flowers,
straightened our ties, sat on the train –
cheap return to Hamilton Central –
      watched them cording you into
space.

The rain clouds parted on cue to let
the sun flood down – I, nearly, believed;
fled to here, got on with this.
          A photograph taken by
accident,
found by chance while searching
for something job-related, petty pap.
      A printout of your mortal grace,
the randomness of a tearing away.

Ticks

Eight-legged ticks stick on to us
as we sweep through grass
in search of the gorge,
a beauty spot sundown, vertigo view.

They hurry, covertly, into our warm bits –
turnups, pockets, zips and folds.

We kill them with our monstrous fingers,
flick them into a different place.
Hurtling away, no questions asked.
Brainlessly blameless, unafraid.

We dodder, cleverly, straight to the edge.

Once before I brought one home;
it fell from my calf when I sat in the bath.

What the fuck is this? I yelped.
A bloodblob nuzzling my Scots-white skin,
a long-haul hitcher doing the crawl.
Indigenous vampire having a laugh.

Small to the Point of Vanishing Entirely

Blackest fathoms. Big pond rim.
   A bucking bronco, Hebrides-style –
a white-knuckle boat trip out to Staffa,
      gripping the rail as we rock and roll.
The skipper brewing-up molten tea,
        first mate cupping a match from the wind,
shaking his head at our rigid grins.
           This could be the place where we die
below the greyly gigantic waves,
but no-one barfs, it's too much fun.
        Soft-eyed seal-lumps watching us bounce,
clown-beaked puffins travelling backwards,
      happy at home in their violent bath.

Magically, out of the fog and scoosh,
      it looms like a Homer enchanted isle.
Fingal's Cave, Mendelssohn's hole.
A bump and a scrape at the landing stage,
   a step from the deck and onto ground.
Strange to be steady, life to be still,
     part of the rise and part of the fall,
the movement of what's in our heads.
        It's easy to slip and open your skull.
This could be the place where we vanish:
      stalks of rock, a fossilised scream
swallowing swell then spewing it out.
   Graceful fulmars gliding the thermals,
        rhythm and chaos, small to the point.
Shape reflections.
   We are here.

Return to the boat and aim for Iona,
                grave of politicians and kings.
The skipper taking a bite from his Twix,
            first mate who'll be dead in a month,
drowned rowing back from a bevvy on Mull,
      lighting another cigarette.
Cormorants perched on spine-bone skerries,
spreading their oil wings, wide to the time.

Remainders

As I heave the hoover gadget about
a tiny whiteness attracts my eye.
I stoop to lift a single whisker
stuck at the foot of the skirting board
beneath the window, in the lounge.
My little cat, dead for years.

Avoiding the housework. All this time
among the crumbs, the skin and fluff,
occasional crispies and shrivelled peas.
Remainders that we never see.
Reminders we are less than perfect,
less than the sum of what we believe.

A finely tapering thread of thin.
It brings it back, the things we slip
as life cleans up; baffling love
for green eyes, a tail, a grape-sized brain.
Instinct signals, redundant words,
a bell round her neck to warn the birds.

It will go in the box that held her ash,
along with her name tag, shred of claw.
Essential, sentimental guff.
Resistance against the unforgiving
sweeping away of everything
that's ever been, will never be.

Could Be a Ford Cortina But It's Hard to Tell

there's a skeleton in the ravine picked clean
           for years
of wing mirrors   headlamps
cushions   dashboard
number plates   nodding dog
           and tyres
which someone took
            the time
   trouble to steal
     ride all the way
to the local beauty spot   set light to
   shove over the top to watch it
roaring   bashing
battering
down

to the bottom
    to rust   rest
        amongst
moss   ferns
   incandescent jungle
which takes the strain
    settles in place   the remains
of another
pushed in long before   a work
of humanity   nature
harmony
     the car
         no longer a car a church
of spiritual metal
left

Squirrels in Space

In the chair   My chair
listening to
       the squirrels
in the space between
             the ceiling   roof

they're up there
scratching   squeaking
scuttling the length of the building
making little squirrels   breathing
inside the cavity
they know

      I'm down here
seething at the ceiling
tapping it with a long handled brush
pressing my face against the window
   trying to see them
        peep out
from the hole in the wood
squeak at the moon   My moon
ignore me   completely
I'm going

      to phone
the pest controllers
        they'll gas them
remove the bodies
block up the hole
      return the space
to total blackness   alone

inside the folds of the mind
       I'll pass
between them
ignore me   completely
leave smudges on the glass

Full Scottish Breakfast

On a useless morning
pudding is cooking
egg is scrambling
nearby
I think

of blue speckled eggs
I stole from a hedge
in the palm of my hand

of stretching   today
across the stump of a tree
with my face up
my sight closed
my tie whipped
across my shoulder as I try
to put it all back   throw it
all back
on a useless morning
bacon is sizzling rings on the stump
turn back to nowhere   now
here   nearby
I think

of summer lawnmower grass
of spinning in sun till I fall
of a knife of apple stuck in my throat

the wind whooshing across my eyes
eggs whooshing around my brain
the first rain
on my skin
as I stretch around my head
and no-one else is anywhere
else   it's me   devouring
the eggs the skin
the breakfast the rings
on a useless morning
toast is burning   nearby
I think

of golliwog badges and goldfish bags
of musical boxes getting slower
and slower
of wasps dying in raspberry jam

soft cobwebs
like a caul
caressing around my face
on a useless morning
with the rain or the sun or the eggs
on an all day morning
the porridge is bubbling
web is caressing
head is frying
nearby   I try
to pull it all out   throw it
all back in to where
the rings turn back to nowhere
else   a first blister
of skin
on my rain

American Civil War

on the carpet
      focused   drawing
hundreds
of little stick men
on top of a hill   on the slopes   in the fields
below   literally
hundreds and hundreds
of blue or grey soldiers   each
in his proper place   no two the same
   a meticulous landscape
of death
   a battle
copied from a bubblegum card
bought from an ice cream van
           playing *Colonel Bogie*
       on the carpet
at my gran's feet
as she watched me
beguiled by my patience
      relentlessly
filling
every inch
of empty paper in gran's house
the piano   sewing machine
net curtains
   scary lampstand
bed settee I'd sleep in
      the glow of the tiny
black and white box
far away
in the corner
          gran   the pencils
              the carpet
drawing
hundreds   hundreds   until
whatever it is is the way
it should be
on the carpet
     focused   drawing

The Life of Fergus in the Hall Cupboard
During the Very Wet Summer of 2007

The highest shelves
are full of dad   objects   such as
a birth certificate in Spanish   a flag
of Chile   a strip of photographs
of a young boy in a sailor suit
smiling up at his father
on a street in Valparaiso   each one
a small epic   a heartbeat more
than the one
before   letters
about an earthquake in 1906
a snowscape in the Andes
a Panama Canal souvenir brochure
stories   still lifes   poems
cigarette cards   film star cards
Brigitte Helm   Loretta Young
bats of the British Isles cards
famous Scottish people cards
David Livingstone   Thomas Carlyle
carefully pasted cowboy scrapbooks
carefully written bicycle diaries
diaries from the war he shouldn't have
kept in case he was captured   killed
without having seen mum
without having made love
without having ridden the pulse
of longing   completion   creation   a ship
in a bottle
made by a German soldier
in exchange for cigarettes and chocolate

I can still smell the cork   pieces clipped
from victory sheets   flowers pressed
in a heavy book   I can still smell
the perfume   letters
about love
threads   a framed picture of a sailing ship
slicing the waves of an imaginary sea
braces   glasses   a shaving razor
the blood plugged with tiny papers
cufflinks   armbands   lists of things
lists of worlds   lists of music he loved
lists of music he needed to love   lists of things
to lift him a heartbeat   more   a letter
he wrote the week before

a death certificate in English   a photograph
of a young boy smiling up at his father
turning into his father
on a hill of ferns in Argyll
who has to make a list of everything
on the highest shelves because
I can no longer be sure of
what he laughed like   what he
sang like   what I look like beneath the dust

**The Death of Fergus on the Kitchen Floor
During the Very Hot Summer of 1976**

Then my dad is lying on his back
still on the linoleum with his eyes
open   milky   not seeing
or seeing clearly   the kitchen he's left
the door into the back garden
the light they say you see   the corridor   light
I'm inches
close to his face   his lips another
colour than normal   I can see
the lips   colour   his eyes   his breath
coming out quickly like he's just run a race
his sleeveless pullover   no glasses on
he always wears glasses
he took them off as if he knew
the television in the background
our neighbour trying to give him mouth to
mouth but not pinching the nose   I tell him
to pinch the nose   calm   the middle
of all   the eye
eyes   the ambulance arrives
and the men do some things on their knees
and shake their heads   look at me
as if to say *do you
think you should be here?*   of course   the end
of the love that made me   linoleum where he
stops   my dad   heart   nose   the only kitchen I
hope to go   whatever I'm trying to find
needing to give a beat of strength   unable
to send a good breath into
the biggest day of my father's   my   life
mum said
he came to her a few nights later
and a voice   not his   said he
wasn't able to speak but was doing okay

The First Memory of Myself in the Sun During the Very Long Summer of 1962

the mile-out sea   flat   silver
          horizon
    everyone running
               further out as I grow
tired   turn without telling
     back the quarter mile
to the sea of people
    ice creams   sandcastles
everyone running   laughing
in the heat   not finding
the place I should be   crying
    through it
for hours
hours   people
saying
what a shame

    the deckchair man
        making me a cup
of tea   greenfly floating
golden   dazzling
tiny wings
a towel on my shoulders
    the sun returns behind
the horizon
balanced
on the handlebars of his big black bike
wobbling along the promenade
to the police station   mum   dad
running in   crying   hugging and
crying a bit more   getting
an ice cream   everything really happy
the deckchair man
   the mile-out sea
         further out as I shrink
alive   behind
the handlebars   big black wings
floating on the   golden   dazzling